JADE JULEP

An Anthology

RITERA PUBLISHING

Jade Julep: An Anthology
Compiled and Edited by: Ritera Publication

ISBN: 978-81-984984-6-5

Preface

In the realm of poetry, words transcend their simple existence, transforming into vessels of emotion, thought, and experience. Each poem is a journey, a glimpse into the soul of its creator, a whisper of truths both personal and universal. **"Jade Julep: An Anthology"** is a celebration of this transformative power of poetry, a curated collection of works from diverse voices, each contributing their unique rhythm and resonance to the symphony of human experience.

As a publisher, we hold a profound privilege to bring together the voices of these talented poets. Their verses span a spectrum of emotions and themes, from the quiet introspection of solitary moments to the vibrant exclamations of love, loss, joy, and everything in between. Each poem in this anthology stands as a testament to the writer's courage in sharing their innermost thoughts and feelings, a beacon of authenticity in a world that often demands conformity.

In these pages, you will find poems that invite you to linger in their quiet beauty, as well as those that challenge you to reflect and rethink. It is my hope that you will discover in this anthology not just the echoes of your own experiences, but also the comforting realization that in our shared humanity, we are never truly alone.

As you turn these pages, may you find solace in the words, inspiration in the verses, and a renewed appreciation for the beauty of the human spirit. Welcome to **"Jade Julep: An Anthology"**—a literary journey into the heart and soul of poetry.

-Ritera Publication

List of Poems

1. To Someone who is Struggling in Silence 7
2. Echoes of the Harvest Gone 13
3. Invisible Strokes 21
4. Sun in Africa 27
5. Happily Ever After 35
6. In the Park, a Father's Prayer 45
7. Price-Less Art 53
8. Whispers through Time 61
9. Daddy's Little Girl 69
10. Embrace the Silence 75

“TO SOMEONE WHO IS STRUGGLING IN SILENCE”

- Shahitha Fareen M

To Someone who's Struggling in Silence

You deserve the world!

Yes, you do.

And by saying "world," I mean all the people who love you unconditionally,

People who wish the best for you,

People who bring out the better in you,

People you're comfortable around,

People with whom you can laugh like an idiot, Yet not feel embarrassed about it!

And remember, in this path of life,

You'll meet people who may bring the worst into your life,

People who manipulate you,

People who make you question your care, honesty, trust, and love.

But you see, they're never permanent!
You can ask, "Why me?"
But oh dear, don't you want to feel;
All kinds of pain, love, tears, anger, sadness, sorrow,
Sympathy, happiness, and much more in this life?

No, you're not in this alone!
Look around; there'll always be a person
Standing quietly in the corner
Just waiting for you to reach their hand to help you!
There always is someone
Believe in me, you, and them!

- Shahitha Fareen M
Writer, Physiotherapist.

***

Synopsis

Shahitha Fareen takes readers on an emotional journey through the highs and lows of life. The poem "To Someone who is Struggling!" is a heartfelt ode to the complexities of human relationships and emotions. It begins with an affirmation, reminding the reader that they deserve all the love and support from those who care for them unconditionally. The poem highlights the importance of surrounding oneself with people who bring out the best in them, those with whom they can share genuine laughter and comfort.

As the poem progresses, it acknowledges the inevitable encounters with individuals who may bring negativity and manipulation into one's life. These experiences, though painful, are portrayed as temporary and essential for personal growth. The poem encourages the reader to embrace the full spectrum of emotions—pain, love, tears, anger, sadness, sorrow, sympathy, and happiness—as they navigate through life.

The poem concludes with a reassuring message that no one is ever truly alone. It emphasizes the presence of supportive individuals who are always there, waiting to lend a helping hand. The poem inspires belief in oneself and in the goodness of others, fostering a sense of hope and resilience.

In essence, "To Someone who is Struggling!" is a celebration of the human experience, urging the reader to cherish the positive relationships in their life while also learning from the challenges they face. It is a reminder that love, support, and understanding are always within reach, even in the darkest of times.

About the Poet

Shahitha Fareen, a multifaceted individual, seamlessly blending her passion for poetry with her professional expertise as a physiotherapist. Born and raised in Tamil nadu, India, Shahitha has always been drawn to the healing arts, both physical and emotional. In addition to her medical career, poetry, rich with emotion and insight, explores themes of healing, resilience, and the beauty of everyday moments.

Shahitha's unique combination of skills allows her to touch lives in multiple ways, whether through the physical relief she provides, or the emotional resonance of her poetry. She continues to inspire many with her dedication to both her crafts, proving that the art of healing can take many forms.

***

“ECHOES OF THE HARVEST GONE”

- Austin Flint

Echoes of the Harvest Gone

In the stillness of a backyard mourn,
Beneath the sky's melancholic hue,
Lie remnants of a summer's scorn,
Where once lush fields in fervor grew.

The sun now casts a solemn gaze,
Upon the withered, lifeless ground,
As whispers of those golden days,
In nature's silent dirge are found.

Each brittle stalk, a testament,
To seasons' cruel and fickle ways,
Yet in their fading, there's a scent,
Of hope that springs from autumn's blaze.

A farmer's hands, so rough and worn,
Cradle dreams within their grasp,
Through drought and storm, they're not yet torn,
With faith that future seeds will clasp.

The earth remembers every tear,
Each seed sown in defiance bold,
In barren times, there's still no fear,
For life within the soil takes hold.

So let the dead crops tell their tale,
Of battles fought and lessons learned,
In every loss, we shall prevail,
For through the ashes, life's fire is burned.

- Austin Flint
Poet.

***

Synopsis

The poem "Echoes of the harvest gone by Austin Flint" is a poignant reflection on the cycles of nature and the resilience of the human spirit. It begins with a somber depiction of a once-vibrant summer now reduced to withered remnants beneath a melancholic sky. The imagery of the sun casting a solemn gaze on the lifeless ground evokes a sense of loss and nostalgia for the golden days of the past.

As the poem progresses, it highlights the harshness of the seasons and the inevitable decay that comes with time. Each brittle stalk serves as a testament to the cruel and fickle ways of nature. However, amidst the fading beauty, there is a glimmer of hope that emerges from the autumn blaze. This hope is embodied in the figure of the farmer, whose rough and worn hands cradle dreams and faith in the future.

The poem emphasizes the farmer's unwavering determination and resilience in the face of adversity. Despite the challenges of drought and storm, the farmer's faith in the potential of future seeds remains unshaken. The earth, too, is portrayed as a living entity that remembers every tear and every seed sown in defiance of barren times.

In the final stanzas, the poem shifts to a message of perseverance and triumph. The dead crops are seen as storytellers of battles fought and lessons learned. The poem concludes with a powerful affirmation that through every loss, there is a prevailing spirit that rises from the ashes, symbolizing the enduring fire of life.

Overall, "Echoes of the Harvest Gone" is a moving exploration of the interplay between nature's cycles and human resilience. It captures the beauty and pain of life's impermanence while celebrating the strength and hope that persist through it all.

***

About the Poet

Austin Flint, an enigmatic soul with an affinity for capturing the melancholic beauty of life's fleeting moments, hails from a small town steeped in agricultural history. With a pen that dances between despair and hope, his evocative verses reflect the rhythms of nature and human experience.

Flint's works often explore themes of resilience, loss, and renewal, drawing inspiration from the landscapes that have both nurtured and challenged him. His poetry resonates with a raw, unfiltered honesty that invites readers to ponder the deeper truths of existence.

***

“INVISIBLE STROKES”

- Stan Miller

Invisible Strokes

In a grand hall, vast and still,
An artist's heart begins to fill.
With colors bright and shadows deep,
A masterpiece, his soul to keep.

No eyes to see, no ears to hear,
Yet in this space, he feels no fear.
Each stroke a dance, each hue a song,
In solitude, where he belongs.

The canvas breathes, the pigments sing,
A silent symphony takes wing.
No audience to praise or scorn,
In this quiet, art is born.

A world within, a dream unfurled,

The artist paints his own new world.

In empty halls, his strokes soars,

Creating beauty, forevermore.

- Stan Miller

Author, Artist.

***

Synopsis

In the vast, silent expanse of a grand hall, an artist stands alone, heart brimming with inspiration. The scene is set with vivid imagery: bright colors and deep shadows, hinting at the masterpiece to come. Without an audience, the artist finds solace in solitude. Each brushstroke becomes a dance, each hue a melody, as he immerses himself in his craft.

The canvas comes alive, breathing and singing with pigments. This silent symphony, free from external judgment, allows the artist to create with pure intention. The absence of praise or scorn liberates him, enabling the birth of true art. The poem beautifully illustrates the internal world of the artist, where dreams take shape and a new world is painted into existence.

In the quiet of the empty hall, the artist's strokes soar, creating timeless beauty. The poem celebrates the power of solitude and the profound connection between the artist and his creation. It emphasizes that true art is born from within, untainted by external influences. "Invisible Strokes" is a tribute to the unseen, yet deeply felt, journey of the artist, highlighting the transformative power of creativity and the enduring legacy of art created in silence.

About the Poet

Stan Miller, a visionary artist and storyteller, resides in the rugged beauty of Western Australia. His days are a kaleidoscope of colors and words, as he captures the essence of the outback on canvas and paper.

Stan's art is a vivid reflection of the landscapes he loves, while his writing delves into the human spirit with profound insight. A true renaissance man, he finds inspiration in the solitude of nature, where he paints and writes with a passion that knows no bounds. In the quiet moments by the sea, Stan's creativity flows, bringing his unique perspective to life.

***

"SUN IN AFRICA"

- Zuri

Sun in Africa

In the heart of Africa,
where the sun blazes bright,
Lies a land of struggle,
yet a beacon of light.

Amidst the shadows of poverty's cruel embrace,
Lives a spirit unbroken,
with an unyielding grace.

Children with eyes,
That tell tales of despair,
Yet dreams in their hearts,
beyond compare.

Mothers who toil from dawn,
Till dusk,
With hands that are calloused,
yet hearts full of trust.

Fathers who labor in fields of dust,
With hopes that tomorrow will bring what it must.

Communities bound by a thread so strong,
In the face of adversity, they sing their song.

For in the depths of hardship,
a fire does burn,
A fighting spirit,
with lessons to learn.

From the slums of Kibera to the deserts of Mali,
Resilience blooms in every alley.
With every sunrise,
a new hope is born,
In the land where the acacia and baobab adorn.

For Africa's heart beats with a rhythm so true,

A testament to the strength that sees them through.

- Zuri
Writer.

***

Synopsis

Zuri pens a vivid picture of Africa's enduring spirit amidst adversity. It begins by acknowledging the continent's challenges, describing it as a land of struggle under the blazing sun. Yet, despite these hardships, Africa is portrayed as a beacon of light, symbolizing hope and resilience.

The poem "SUN IN AFRICA" highlights the unbroken spirit and unyielding grace of its people. Children's eyes reflect tales of despair, yet their hearts harbor dreams beyond compare, illustrating the hope that persists even in the youngest generations. Mothers and fathers are depicted laboring tirelessly, their calloused hands and dusty fields representing the physical toll of their work. Despite these challenges, they maintain trust and hope for a better tomorrow.

Communities are described as being bound by a strong thread, singing their song in the face of adversity. This metaphor emphasizes the unity and resilience that characterize African societies. The poem suggests that within hardship lies a burning fire—a fighting spirit that imparts valuable lessons.

Geographical references, from the slums of Kibera to the deserts of Mali, underscore the widespread nature of this resilience across the continent. The imagery of resilience blooming in every alley suggests that hope and strength emerge even in the most challenging environments.

The poem concludes by celebrating the renewal of hope with each sunrise in a land adorned by acacia and baobab trees, symbols of Africa's natural beauty and endurance. The beating heart of Africa is portrayed as having a true rhythm, a testament to the strength that sustains its people through adversity.

Overall, the poem is a tribute to the resilience, unity, and enduring hope of the African people, highlighting their capacity to find light amidst darkness and strength in the face of challenges.

***

About the Poet

Zuri, a distinguished poet of African descent, weaves her verses with the threads of poverty and the indomitable spirit of her people. Her poetry, rich in imagery and profound in its depth, captures the stark realities of life while celebrating the resilience and hope that define the human spirit. Through her eloquent and evocative lines, Zuri seeks to illuminate the socio-economic challenges faced by many, urging her audience towards empathy and action.

Her work stands as a testament to her unwavering commitment to justice and equality, reflecting a deep connection to her heritage. Zuri's literary contributions continue to inspire and uplift, making her a beacon of hope and a voice for the voiceless.

***

"HAPPILY EVER AFTER"

- Saran Raj

Happily Ever After

I left behind all my belongings,
Just to reach you with pure love.
Sorry, babe, I lied---
It's just the shovel, a piece to reach my love.

The sun dips below the horizon,
No one can see us kiss.
Sorry, babe,
For spoiling your lip gloss, I'll buy a new one

I can smell your hair,
Through the thin air.
Sorry, babe, for the odour—
It's just the sweat; we'll forget it out of love.

My eyes turned red,

Since the day you left.

Sorry, babe, for skipping the meds—

I'll rest in your arms now, scratch my head, like you always do, my love.

I'm not crying,

It's just the showers.

Sorry, babe, I lied—

It's my tears, and I don't want to drench you in them, my love.

Do you remember the frogs and bees,

Back in our garden?

They sang for you all night, since you left---

And it was me in the daytime, for you my love.

Fuckin napkins were gone,

Really gone.

Sorry, babe, I used your skirt—

Just to save your picture from the tears of your love.

My show will take place in a while,

My agony will be gone in a while.

Sorry, babe,

I can't pull the crowd; it's just you and me, my love.

Is it worth it without you, my love?

I questioned my existence.

Sorry, babe,

The answer I was looking for—it was you, my love.

This drug isn't working,

I don't know why.

All I feel is getting closer to you—

With all my heart, my love.

Divine and grace is what I feel,

By getting closer every inch,

I'm the happiest man in the world,

I see you sprinting towards me,

I'm gonna drop this California poppies,

Pen, paper, and my breathe altogether, On your feet--

As always I loved to stay,

Hug me tight,

As closer you can, as tighter you can,

My hands tremble, I don't feel my body,

Where were you my love,

I was worried,

Hold my hands, and never.........

- Saran Raj
Author.

***

Synopsis

Saran Raj's poem "Happily Ever After" delves into the profound depths of grief and longing, echoing themes prevalent in classical poetry.

The poem opens with the narrator abandoning all possessions, symbolizing a detachment from the material world in pursuit of a love that transcends earthly bounds. The mention of a shovel subtly introduces the motif of mortality, suggesting a willingness to confront death to reunite with the beloved.

As the sun sets, creating a private, intimate atmosphere, the narrator reflects on past moments of closeness, expressing regret for minor transgressions like smudging lip gloss. This evokes a sense of cherished memories now tinged with sorrow. The sensory imagery of smelling the beloved's hair through the air underscores the deep connection that persists despite physical separation.

The transformation of the narrator's eyes to red signifies prolonged weeping and the physical manifestations of grief. Neglecting medication highlights the depth of despair, with a yearning to find solace in the memory of the beloved's comforting gestures, such as head scratches.

Tears are metaphorically described as showers, a natural outpouring of sorrow that the narrator wishes to conceal to protect the beloved from further pain. Recalling shared experiences, like the frogs and bees in their garden serenading the beloved, emphasizes the profound sense of loss and the void left behind.

In a poignant moment, the narrator uses the beloved's skirt to protect a picture from tears, symbolizing a desperate attempt to preserve memories amidst overwhelming grief. The anticipation of an upcoming "show" reflects the narrator's internal struggle, acknowledging that without the beloved, any endeavor feels devoid of meaning.

The poem delves into existential contemplation, with the narrator questioning their purpose in the absence of their love. The realization that the beloved was the answer to their existence deepens the sense of emptiness and despair.

Turning to substances for relief proves futile, as the narrator finds themselves feeling closer to the beloved, suggesting a desire to transcend the physical realm to reunite. This proximity brings a sense of divine grace, making the narrator feel like the happiest person alive.

The last few stanza portrays a vivid vision of the beloved approaching, prompting the narrator to abandon earthly possessions—California poppies, pen, paper—and even their breath at the beloved's feet. This act signifies a complete surrender, a longing to be embraced tightly, as the narrator's physical sensations wane.

The poem concludes with a haunting question about the beloved's absence, revealing the narrator's profound worry and a plea for eternal togetherness. The unfinished phrase "Hold my hands, and never..." leaves readers in suspense, emphasizing the narrator's desperation for an unending union.

The darkness of the poem lies in its unflinching portrayal of grief's consuming nature and the narrator's contemplation of mortality as a means to reunite with the lost beloved. This mirrors the somber tones of classical elegies, where poets grapple with the finality of death and the enduring pain of loss.

"Happily Ever After" is a deeply moving exploration of love, loss, and the consuming nature of grief. Its themes and tone resonate with classical poetry, offering a timeless reflection on the human condition and the enduring impact of losing a beloved.

***

About the Author

Saran Raj is an Indian author known for his insightful works on themes like parenting, mental health, and discrimination. His book "Someday Perhaps: Hoping For A Change" addresses these complex issues through real-life experiences, offering readers a deep understanding of these topics. Another notable work is "Twined Echoes," a psychological romantic-comedy novel that explores relationships and self- discovery.

Saran Raj's writing style is characterized by its simplicity and emotional resonance, making his stories relatable and impactful. He has a unique ability to connect with readers on a personal level, encouraging them to reflect on their own lives and the world around them.

His dedication to addressing important social issues through his writing has earned him a critical acclaim. His works continue to inspire and resonate with readers, making him a significant figure in contemporary Indian literature.

***

"IN THE PARK, A FATHER'S PRAYER"

- Frank Gilmore

In the Park, A Father's Prayer

Beneath the azure sky so wide,
A father walks with gentle pace,
Beside his son, their worlds collide,
In laughter, love, and fleeting grace.

The child's eyes gleam with pure delight,
As swings and slides his joy embrace,
Yet in the father's heart a fight,
For future trials his son may face.

These moments, sweet and undisturbed,
Hold whispers of the years to come,
A father's love, so deeply stirred,
By thoughts of what his child becomes.

Will he be strong, in chaos bold?
Will kindness guide him through the fray?
These questions in the father's hold,
As shadows cast on bright today.

But for now, he treasures each smile,
Each giggle in the sunlit park,
Hoping to shield, though just a while,
His son from world's impending dark.

- Frank Gilmore
Writer.

***

Synopsis

Frank Gilmore's poem, "In the Park, A Father's Prayer," explores the deep bond between a father and his son on a peaceful day at the park. Set against a large, beautiful sky, the story follows a father's introspective journey as he observes his child's simple joy amidst playground activity. The poem begins with images of a wide azure sky beneath which the father and son walk together. The term "their worlds collide" refers to the merger of the father's adult perceptions and the child's pure innocence. As the child enjoys the joys of swings and slides, his eyes glitter with unadulterated enjoyment, causing the father to smile and reflect.

While the child is playing, the father is concerned about his son's future. He considers the obstacles that lie ahead, and wonders if his son will have the strength and generosity required to negotiate life's complications. These reflections create a pall over the present moment, emphasizing the father's deepest concerns and wishes.

Despite these concerns, the father is well aware of the transient nature of their current situation. He appreciates each grin and laugh exchanged in the sunlit park, knowing that these are only momentary respites from life's inevitable sorrows. His wish to hide his son from the world's impending troubles exemplifies the inherent parental drive to keep one's child safe.

The poem's structure contrasts the child's carefree enjoyment with the father's contemplative concerns, successfully depicting the difference between juvenile innocence and mature responsibility. This interplay underlines the bittersweet truth of parenting: the thrill of seeing a child happy while also anticipating their future hardships. In essence, "In the Park, A Father's Prayer" captures the delicate balance between enjoying the current moment and facing future uncertainties. Frank Gilmore depicts a father's tremendous love and the underlying conflict between appreciating the present and fearing the unknown with beautiful imagery and emotional depth. The poem is a moving reminder of the fleeting beauty of life's moments and the eternal power of parental concern.

***

About the Poet

Frank Gilmore is a poet whose works often delve into the tender and deep aspects of parenthood and the passage of time. Drawing from his own experiences as a father, Gilmore's poetry captures the bittersweet moments that define the journey of raising a child.

His verses are marked by a deep sense of empathy and introspection, exploring the hopes and fears that come with guiding a young soul through life. Gilmore's poignant storytelling and vivid imagery resonate with readers, offering a heartfelt glimpse into the complexities of love and family.

***

“PRICE-LESS ART”

- Vishnu K. Prasanna

Price-less Art

In the dim-lit attic,
Shadows wove his days,
A brush, a palette,
In solitary gaze.

His wallet empty, dreams filled his heart,
For a canvas and colors, he played his part.
With torn clothes, and eyes lit with fire,
He painted his passion, his one desire.

The world outside, cold and unforgiving,
Yet in art's embrace, he found his living.
One day she came, like a whisper soft,
To pose for a picture, in light aloft.

Her beauty simple, pure and bright,
She became his muse, his guiding light.
Her laughter echoed, in his heart confined,
Her presence an anchor, to a soul entwined.

He painted her essence, her spirit, her grace,
In every stroke, her visage he traced.
Though pockets were bare, his love was whole,
For art and her, he bared his soul.

They lived through poverty, strife, and pain,
Yet together they stood, in sunshine and rain.
For money fades, and riches depart,
But art and love, reside in the heart.

In the world of canvas, dreams unfurled,
A poor artist, and his muse, against the world.

- Vishnu K. Prasanna
Poet, Student.

Synopsis

Price-less Art by Vishnu K. Prasanna is a heartfelt poem that explores the life of a struggling artist who finds comfort and purpose in his craft. Set in a dimly lit attic, the poem paints a vivid picture of the artist's solitary existence, where shadows define his days, and his dreams fill his heart despite an empty wallet. The artist's passion for painting is evident as he continues to create, even with torn clothes and eyes lit with fire.

The world outside is depicted as cold and unforgiving, yet the artist finds his living in the embrace of his art. His life takes a turn when a woman enters his world, like a whisper soft, to pose for a picture. Her simple, pure beauty and bright presence become his muse and guiding light. Her laughter echoes in his heart, anchoring his soul and intertwining their lives.

The artist captures her essence, spirit, and grace in every stroke, baring his soul through his art. Despite their poverty and the strife they endure, their love remains whole and unwavering. They stand together through sunshine and rain, finding strength in each other and their shared passion for art.

The poem beautifully contrasts the transient nature of money and riches with the enduring power of art and love. It emphasizes that while material wealth may fade, the true treasures of life reside in the heart. The artist and his muse, though poor in worldly possessions, are rich in their love and dedication to their craft.

In the world of canvas, their dreams unfurl, and they stand united against the world. "Price-less Art" is a moving tribute to the resilience of the human spirit, the transformative power of love, and the timeless beauty of art.

***

About the Poet

Vishnu K. Prasanna, a gifted poet from Kerala who finds joy in weaving words into captivating verses. His poetry spans a wide range of themes, from the beauty of nature to the depths of human emotions.

With a pen in hand, Vishnu explores love, resilience, and identity, blending tradition with modernity. Poetry is not just a hobby for Vishnu; it's a lifelong passion. His reflective and observational nature shines through in his works.

***

“WHISPERS THROUGH TIME”

- Jordan Silk

Whispers Through Time

In days when skies were clear and bright,
You held me close with love's pure light.
But now the clouds have cast their shade,
And memories begin to fade.

With gentle hands, you combed my hair,
In every strand, your tender care.
But now those hands, they tremble so,
In worlds where only shadows grow.

Your eyes once sparkled, knowing me,
Now search the room, where could I be?
Yet in your gaze, a distant star,
I hope you see me from afar.

Each whispered name, a fragile thread,
Connecting hearts, though words have fled.
Though time may weave its silent maze,
In your embrace, my heart still stays.

For every lost and broken thought,
A lifetime's love, so dearly bought.
I hold you close, though time may steal,
The moments that we used to feel.

So here I stand, a brother true,
In honor of the love we knew.
A gentle whisper through the years,
A mother's love that perseveres.

- Jordan Silk
Writer.

Synopsis

Whispers Through Time" penned by Jordan Silk, offering an intimate portrayal of a son's experience as he watches his mother slowly succumb to the devastating effects of Alzheimer's disease. This heart-wrenching piece captures the slow, painful unraveling of his mother's memories, reflecting on the irreversible changes that come with the passage of time and the cruel toll of illness. Silk's use of vivid, sensory- driven imagery, paired with tender and poignant expressions, allows the reader to feel the son's deep sense of loss and helplessness as his mother slips further away from him, her identity increasingly obscured by the shadows of the disease.

At its core, the poem delves into the bittersweet nature of love, exploring how it persists despite the ravages of time and the encroachment of illness. Silk portrays the bond between mother and child as one that is not easily broken, even as the mother's recognition and memories fade. It speaks to the emotional complexity of caregiving, the delicate balance between remembering and letting go, and the challenge of maintaining connection when memory itself is lost.

"Whispers Through Time" is more than just an expression of sorrow; it is a poignant celebration of the enduring strength of love and family. Through the pain of watching a loved one slip away, the poem highlights the resilience and unwavering commitment that define familial ties. The enduring bond between mother and son, even in the absence of shared memories, is a testament to the powerful and timeless nature of love, transcending even the harshest of circumstances. Silk's heartfelt ode serves as a reminder that while time may erode memories, it cannot diminish the unbreakable force of love, compassion, and the deep connections that tie us to one another.

***

About the Poet

Jordan Silk, a poet with a heart attuned to life's tender moments, grew up in the embrace of his mother's care. His work often explores the themes of memory and love, weaving personal experiences into universal emotions.

Inspired by his family's journey through his mother's battle with Alzheimer's, Jordan's poetry resonates with empathy and hope. He believes in the power of words to heal and connect. Through his verses, he honors the enduring bonds that time cannot sever.

***

"DADDY'S LITTLE GIRL"

- Zain Al Fakri

Daddy's Little Girl

In the quiet dawn, they set sail,
Father and daughter, hand in hand,
Across the border of their homeland,
Where the sea whispers secrets of serenity.

No worries weigh their hearts,
No agony clouds their minds,
Just the gentle rhythm of the waves,
And the promise of a peaceful journey.

The horizon stretches wide and free,
A canvas of endless possibilities,
Where dreams drift like the morning mist,
And hope dances on the water's edge.

Their laughter mingles with the breeze,
A melody of love and trust,
As they navigate the open sea,
Bound by an unspoken bond.

The sun rises, painting the sky,
With hues of gold and amber light,
Pushing them towards a new horizon,
Where peace and tranquility reside.

In this moment, we are infinite,
Me and my dad, side by side,
Sailing through the border of our homeland,
With hearts unburdened, and spirits light.

- Zain Al Fakri
Activist, Poet.

***

Synopsis

In this evocative poem, a father and daughter embark on a serene journey at dawn, hand in hand, as they leave behind their birthplace. The gentle waves of the sea and the promise of a pleasant voyage soothe their hearts, creating a sense of tranquility. As they sail, their laughter and unspoken bond form a melody of love and trust, highlighting the deep connection between them.

The rising light paints the sky in hues of gold and amber, symbolizing a new horizon filled with endless possibilities. This moment of boundless connection brings them a sense of calm and lightness, as they sail together with free hearts. The poem beautifully captures the essence of their journey, emphasizing the importance of love, trust, and the shared experience of exploring new beginnings.

Through vivid imagery and heartfelt expressions, the poem portrays the father and daughter's journey as a metaphor for life's adventures and the enduring bond between loved ones. The peaceful setting of the sea and the rising light serve as a backdrop for their emotional journey, reflecting the beauty of their relationship and the hope for a bright future.

In essence, Zain pens a celebration of the unbreakable bond between a father and daughter, their shared moments of joy, and the promise of new beginnings. It reminds us of the power of love and trust to guide us through life's journeys, no matter where they may lead.

About the Poet

Zain Al Fikri, a budding poet residing in the heart of Beirut, Lebanon. With a soul deeply intertwined with the rich tapestry of his homeland, Zain's verses echo the timeless beauty and profound history of Lebanon. His poetry, a harmonious blend of classical elegance and contemporary insight, captures the essence of human experience and the enduring spirit of his people.

When not immersed in his literary pursuits, Zain can be found wandering the ancient streets of Beirut, drawing inspiration from its storied past and vibrant present. His work is a testament to the power of words to transcend time and space, offering readers a glimpse into the soul of a poet who finds beauty in every corner of his beloved city.

***

“EMBRACE THE SILENCE”

- Julia Shade

Embrace The Silence

In quiet nights where shadows dance,
A soul finds peace in solitude,
With every breath, a silent trance,
Alone, yet never destitute.

The void, a canvas vast and pure,
Where thoughts can wander, unconfined,
In stillness, one begins to cure,
The restless heart, the troubled mind.

No voices break the tranquil air,
No chaos mars the silent sphere,
In nothingness, there's beauty rare,
A space where clarity draws near.

Each moment spent in silent grace,
Is filled with whispers of the soul,
In solitude, one finds a place,
Where broken parts become a whole.

The world outside may roar and fight,
But in the quiet, joy is found,
For in the heart of darkest night,
A gentle peace in void is crowned.

- Julia Shade
Author, Artist.

***

Synopsis

Embrace of Silence by Julia Shade is a serene meditation on the joys of solitude and the profound peace found in embracing the void. Through delicate and introspective language, the poem captures the quiet beauty of being alone and the clarity that comes from within. Shade's verses depict a soul at ease in the stillness, finding solace and healing in the absence of external noise. Each stanza reflects the tranquil journey of self-discovery and the serenity that emerges from solitude, celebrating the inner peace that arises when one embraces the emptiness.

In this poem, Shade masterfully uses imagery and metaphor to convey the essence of solitude. The "void" is not portrayed as a negative space, but rather as a canvas for introspection and personal growth. The absence of external distractions allows the speaker to connect with their inner self, leading to a deeper understanding of their own thoughts and emotions.

The poem's structure and rhythm mirror the calm and steady pace of a meditative state. Each line flows seamlessly into the next, creating a sense of continuity and harmony.

Shade's choice of words evokes a sense of tranquility, with phrases like "quiet beauty" and "stillness" emphasizing the peaceful nature of solitude.

As the poem progresses, the reader is invited to join the speaker on their journey of self-discovery. The "healing" mentioned in the poem refers to the emotional and mental rejuvenation that comes from spending time alone. In the stillness, the speaker finds clarity and a renewed sense of purpose.

Ultimately, "Embrace of Silence" is a celebration of the inner peace that can be found when one embraces solitude. It encourages readers to appreciate the moments of quiet in their lives and to use them as opportunities for reflection and growth. Shade's poem serves as a reminder that solitude is not something to be feared, but rather a gift that can lead to profound personal insights and a deeper connection with oneself.

***

About the Poet

Julia Shade is a contemplative poet whose works explore the depths of solitude and the beauty of the inner world. Her verses are characterized by their introspective nature, capturing the nuances of quiet moments and the serenity found in stillness.

Drawing inspiration from her own experiences with solitude, Shade's poetry offers a profound meditation on the joys of being alone and the clarity that arises from embracing the void. Her writing resonates with those who seek solace in reflection and the quiet spaces of life.

***

To our incredible authors,

Your words have woven a tapestry of emotions, capturing the essence of silence, personal void, pain, the struggle of artists, poverty, chaos in the world, and illness. Your contributions to **"Jade Julep: An Anthology"** have not only enriched this collection but have also provided solace and understanding to those who seek comfort in the written word.

Thank you for sharing your profound insights and for being a part of this journey. Your dedication and talent have made this anthology a beacon of hope and empathy.

With deepest gratitude
Ritera Publication.

About Us

Welcome to the world of "Jade Julep: An Anthology," a captivating collection of stories, poems, and essays that celebrate the diverse voices and experiences of authors fromaround the globe. Our anthology is a testament to the power of storytelling and the magic that happens when creativity knows no bounds.

Who We Are

We Ritera, a self-publishing house with a mission to empower authors and bring their unique voices to the forefront. With a presence in over 150 countries, we have helpedcountless writers overcome the challenges of the publishing world and share their stories with readers everywhere. Our team is dedicated to providing the support andresources needed to turn your writing dreams into reality.

Our Journey

Ritera's began with a simple idea: to create a platform where authors could thrive andconnect with readers on a global scale. Over the years, we have grown into a vibrant community of writers, editors, and literary enthusiasts who share a passion for the written word. "Jade Julep: An Anthology" is the culmination of our efforts, showcasing the incredible talent and creativity of our authors.

Our Mission

At the heart of our publishing house is a commitment to fostering a supportive and inclusive environment for writers. We believe that every story deserves to be told, andwe are dedicated to helping authors navigate the complexities of the publishing process. From manuscript development to marketing and distribution, we provide comprehensive services to ensure your work reaches its full potential.

***

Acknowledgements

We extend our deepest gratitude to **Ratix Info Tech** for their exceptional work ontheinterior design and cover design of this book. Their creativity and dedication have truly brought **"Jade Julep: An Anthology"** to life, making it a visual delight for our readers. Thank you for your invaluable contribution to this project.

***

9 788198 498465

Printed at Repro India Ltd.